PURPOSE IN THE
FOURTH QUARTER

Comments From
Some in the Fourth Quarter

"Bernie Brown has served as a member and chair of the Tommy Nobis Center Board. Though his football knowledge is good, his understanding of the game of life is even better. I agree with him; life, like football, is about winning. *Purpose in the Fourth Quarter* explains what winning means."

-Tommy Nobis, Two time All-American, University of Texas; NFL Rookie of the Year 1966 and five time Pro Bowler – Atlanta Falcons; Founder of the Tommy Nobis Center

★★★★★★★★★

"When contemplating retirement, I had a colleague comment, "When you retire you won't be a doctor anymore!" I hadn't thought about the way many of us put our whole selves into our occupations to the exclusion of other important aspects of life. Bernie Brown reminds us of the significance of each quarter and particularly that final one. We each will gain from pausing to consider the true purpose of our 'game of life'."

-Donald Mosley, M.D., Cardiologist, Louisville, KY (retired after practicing 30 years to study and promote medical ethics); Board of Directors of several charitable organizations

★★★★★★★★★

"As we press on toward the goal (a purposeful life) to win the prize… (Philippians 3:14), Bernie Brown offers insight for living a full and victorious fourth quarter. Furthermore, *Purpose in the Fourth Quarter* will bless you with advice and counsel regardless of where you are in the game of life. Bernie invites you to have a conversation with him; I've had many. You will enjoy and profit from it."

-Dr. Robert Bowling, United Methodist Minister (retired after forty one years in fulltime ministry); Recipient, Harry Denman Evangelism Award

★★★★★★★★★★

"Like a painting that is not completed until the final stroke of a brush, Bernie Brown reminds us that the game of life is not over until the last quarter has ended. Bernie has been a blessing to our family for over fifty years, and I have always valued his wise counsel. Read *Purpose in the Fourth Quarter*; you will see what I mean!"

-Annette Rigdon Swan, Professional Artist and Retired Art Teacher (still painting in her nineties); Author's Mother-in-law

PURPOSE IN THE
FOURTH QUARTER

FINISHING THE GAME OF LIFE VICTORIOUSLY

BERNIE BROWN

Inspiring Voices®

A Service of Guideposts

Inspiring Voices books may be ordered through booksellers or by contacting:

Inspiring Voices
1663 Liberty Drive
Bloomington, IN 47403
www.inspiringvoices.com
1-(866) 697-5313

ISBN: 978-1-4624-0286-1 (sc)
ISBN: 978-1-4624-0285-4 (e)

Library of Congress Control Number: 2012946691

Printed in the United States of America

Inspiring Voices rev. date: 09/13/2012

This book is dedicated to one of the most beloved women that I have ever known. She demonstrated purpose in every quarter, but especially in the fourth. She was my role model and encouraged me in this effort. She claimed victory two weeks after the completion of this work.

To my mom, **Elizabeth Brown,** 1919–2012.

CONTENTS

FOREWORD

Football has played a very significant role in my life. As a player and coach, I have always felt that many lessons in life can be learned on the football field. In fact, I believed that my coaching job was not only to help develop athletic skills, but more importantly, to instill principles and values in our players that will serve them well for a lifetime.

Even though I played and coached for many years, I did not make the connection that is conveyed in this interesting and thought-provoking book. It points out how the game of life has so many similarities to the game of football...four quarters, a half-time and sometimes even overtime. And, there is little doubt that the fourth quarter in a football game is the most demanding, intense and exciting period; its conclusion ends the game in either victory or defeat.

Despite the fact that Bernie Brown played very little football, he has grasped the essence of these two games – football and life. Being a Christian, he also accurately identifies the true purpose of each – winning. By using a conversational style, he allows you to participate and gain understanding of the game of life's progression, interruptions, score-keeping and ultimate purpose - victory.

For you fourth quarterers (like me) who read this, special insight and renewed enthusiasm can be gained from pondering its offerings. In my opinion, *Purpose in the Fourth Quarter* needs to be in your hands and not on your shelf! As Bernie says, "It can at least start you thinking and at best have a positive influence on you at this point in your life."

We all could be well served by adding this little volume to our "playbooks."

Raymond Berry
All-NFL Wide Receiver – Baltimore Colts
Head Coach - New England Patriots (Super Bowl
XX)
Pro Football Hall of Fame

PREFACE

To me, a *preface* is a little different from an introduction. The preface sets forth the purpose of the work whereas the introduction *introduces* the ideas that are to follow. I like to think of it as the *pre-face*. *Pre* means something that is coming before the main thing, and *face* means looking directly toward something. Therefore, my purpose here is to get you ready to look at something. And I believe that this particular *something* can at least start you thinking and at best have a positive influence on you at this point in your life.

As I write this, my mother is ninety-three years old and living in a skilled nursing facility. She is deep in the fourth quarter. While I was visiting with her one day, I began thinking about the tremendous impact that she has had on my life. Then my mind became focused on the influence that her entire generation had on my generation. In addition to my mom, I thought of my dad, father-in-law, mother-in-law, aunts, uncles, and even older friends—both deceased and still with us. I just wanted to thank them but didn't know how. For some reason, the following verses came to me, even though I'm certainly not a poet. I offer this as my preface and in appreciation to that generation that raised me: *the greatest generation.* They helped me find purpose at various stages of my life.

A Time to Run

There is a time when you've yet to run,
And you feel that day will never come.
You crawl, then walk, and at last you run.
The race of life has just begun!

★★★★★★★★★★

There is a time when you enjoy the run,
And you sense your turn has finally come.
You leap at the sound of the starting gun.
The race begun seems easily won.

★★★★★★★★★★

There is a time when you only run,
And you wonder what you have become.
Days lack meaning at every turn.
This race through life is far less fun!

★★★★★★★★★★

There is a time when you cannot run,
And you fear that your days will flee.
Then you hear, "Though you cannot run,
You can walk or just talk with me."

★★★★★★★★★★

There is a time when you cease to run,
Or walk or talk or see.
Then the gates open and you'll hear,
"Well done,
Now run, my child, run to me." [1]

As we live our lives, I truly believe that an inherent need for *purpose* exists within each one of us. I would go so far as to say that purpose is one of the main keys to fulfillment, joy, and true success. The discussion that follows is my attempt to help you find *purpose* wherever you are along your life's journey. Special emphasis will be placed on the fourth quarter of life where I presently reside; however, we will pass through the other three to get there.

In an effort to make this as meaningful as possible, I am imagining that you and I are sitting in my den and having a friendly conversation. Therefore, much is written in the first-person point of view. You will hear what I have to say, and at the end of each chapter, you will have your say by answering the questions to give your perspective on this game of life that we all are playing.

Welcome to my home. It's great to meet you. Thanks for joining me!

INTRODUCTION

At a recent Christian Writers Fellowship meeting that I attend periodically, we were asked, "Why do you write?" I had no good answer that day but have given it some thought. The reason I write is the same reason I talk: I have a need to share something that I believe to be significant in this game called life. This desire seems to become even more important to me as I have gotten older. I am now in my seventies and have played out much of my game of life on this earth. To be honest, I am probably putting these ideas in writing more for myself than for those of you who might honor me by taking the time to read them. Writing helps me organize my thoughts and solidify my beliefs, which are two things I feel the need to do particularly at this stage. I hope and pray that this may be more helpful than anything that I have ever written and shared in the past. I can say this without apology because much of it comes from listening to others. For the past year or so, I have been asking individuals and groups, "What is your purpose at this point in your life?"

I became most intrigued with this question when Snookie, my wife, and I were asked to lead an older-adult retreat awhile back; our subject was "Purpose in the Fourth Quarter." The group was a perfect size—neither too large nor too small. The participation was unbelievable. I was told later that in the small breakout groups, some people who never say anything opened up not only their mouths, but also their hearts. Several notes from the participants were very encouraging. One stated, "I've attended many senior retreats but none have touched me as much as this one." My conclusion is that this subject, "Purpose in the Fourth Quarter," is on the minds and hearts of many people. Subsequently, from my informal research, I have also learned that *purpose in all quarters* is something we all desire, regardless of our place in the game of life.

When I think of games with four quarters, my mind automatically goes to football. I didn't play football. On the other hand, yes, I did! I was on a junior high team and played in a club league one year; I even played flag football for my fraternity in college. So I guess that I can claim some expertise on this wonderful game that has almost gained religious status in my home region: the South. And I'm an avid fan!

Certainly, I could have chosen another sport as my illustration. Tennis, for instance, was my passion during college and afterward. And golf became my second athletic focus a little later in life, after my joints began to bother me. However, tennis consists of three to five sets and golf requires completion of eighteen holes, neither of which seems to fit the analogy that I was attempting to make concerning the game of life.

Football has four quarters with a half-time break in the middle, and similarly, I believe that the game of life can easily fit into the same time sequence. But like other sports, though football has its own unique features, the bottom line in the game is winning. The goal is to win! Some may disagree, but I firmly believe that the bottom line in the game of life is also winning. The goal is to win! I hope that we can explore together both football and life to gain a better understanding of victorious living.

In this book, I will be sharing many thoughts gained from others and even a few of my own. But my challenge is for you to gain an understanding of your purpose—no, *God's* purpose—for your life. You see, we are "called according to His purpose"!

Chapter 1

THE GAME OF FOOTBALL

ON THE SURFACE, THE game of football is relatively simple. Two teams play the game for an hour, and the one that scores the most points wins. There are four fifteen-minute quarters, during which the players attempt to score as many points as possible. The teams are also alternately playing defense, attempting to prevent or limit scoring by the other team. The game is played at many levels, and the rules vary a bit among the leagues, but the playing principles are basically the same. I enjoy high school football, like college the most, and am less enthusiastic about the professional game. My wife actually dislikes pro football because she describes it as "a bunch of older men playing a boy's game." She says this takes the fun out of it.

Though the game seems simple on the surface, I tried to imagine what it would be like to take a friend from a foreign country to see an American football game. My guess is that he would at best be very confused and most probably totally befuddled as he watched. From such a perspective, you will quickly conclude this game is very complex and demanding. To further confirm this, our society handsomely rewards those who take this game seriously and attempt to perfect the playing of it.

Here are a few of the factors that make this game highly complicated yet intriguing:

> *A football has an awkward shape.* If you think about it, most balls used in various sports are round. A leather football has a pointed, oval shape. This allows it to spiral when it is kicked or passed, but it also causes the ball to take crazy and unexpected bounces when fumbled or loose. The outcomes of some games have even been affected by the bounce of such a ball.
>
> *Football is one of the true team sports.* Eleven players on both the offensive and defensive sides of the ball confront each other in physical combat. Each player has a unique role that will help determine the outcome of each play. Teammates on the field must be continuously engaged and depend on each other for success.
>
> *There are multiple ways to score.* Though points are typically scored by touchdowns and extra points, other means are available to increase a team's score. A three-point field

goal is another alternative. There are two other ways to score, and both are for two points. First, there is a two-point conversion ("going for two") after a touchdown. And second is a safety, which is the result of a player being tackled in his own end zone by the defensive team. The fact that there are multiple ways to score adds to the strategic decision-making process throughout the game.

Plans may change at the last second. Offensive plays are predetermined and communicated to the entire team while in the huddle or through audible signals outside the huddle. As the signals are barked out by the quarterback, he may decide to change the original play after viewing the defense. Great quarterbacks read defenses well, while great defensive teams anticipate offensive moves. It is a fluid and dynamic game constantly requiring changes and adjustments.

Size, strength, speed, and other physical as well as mental attributes dictate positions. Offensive as well as defensive linemen tend to be very large and strong; receivers and defensive backs must be especially fast with good hand-eye coordination; running backs have speed, strength, and agility; kickers need strong legs; and quarterbacks must not only have athletic ability but also be

3

mentally astute. In other words, the gifts possessed by individual team members usually determine their respective positions on the team.

Defense wins games. I don't exactly understand this, but many successful coaches at various levels have told me this is a fact. It doesn't mean good offense is unnecessary, but if you can keep the other team from scoring, you will inevitably be a winner.

Having the best players does not always ensure victory. In college, a player's eligibility to play is limited to four years. If successful, however, coaches remain a constant, leading influence for many years. The leadership of coaches probably contributes more to a victorious program than any other component. The team's fans, student body, band, cheerleaders, and mascots can inspire and motivate while disrupting the opponent, particularly on a home field. Due to numerous factors, teams with less talent will often be victorious over those with more.

The length of each fifteen-minute quarter will vary. You would think that fifteen minutes are always fifteen minutes. But in a football game, many factors can cause the clock to stop, causing the actual time to be lengthened. Here are a few events that hold time: time-outs, penalties, injuries, going out of bounds, incomplete passes, first downs, touchdowns, lightning strikes, and, if televised, commercial breaks.

★★★★★★★★★★

You would think that fifteen minutes are always fifteen minutes.

★★★★★★★★★★

These arc just a few interesting characteristics of the game of football. It would take a complete book to explore them all.

With this, we'll leave the athletic field. I ask you to join me in another arena where a different game is being played. However, the goal is the same: victory! Share your thoughts by answering the following questions.

"If anyone completes as an athlete (in the **game**), he does not receive the victor's crown unless he competes according to the rules" (2 Timothy 2:5).

The Game of Football – Self-Analysis

1. What is your definition of a game?

2. Are you a football fan? If so, what do you enjoy most about the game?

3. What are some other aspects of the game of football not cited in the chapter that make it unique and exciting?

4. Does a sport such as football teach lessons that are helpful in life? If so, name some.

5. Do you think God takes sides in a football game? Does He care who wins? Explain your opinion.

Chapter 2

THE GAME OF LIFE

IS IT ACCURATE, FAIR, or even appropriate to call life a game? What is a game? Dictionaries have some interesting definitions: sport, fun, amusement, contest, a field of gainful activity. Another definition was "the game of chance" in which luck is the chief factor in determining the winner. Some may claim that all of these play out in the game of life. We will see! But for the sake of our discussion here, let's at least agree that life has some characteristics of a "game."

I contend that life is a game, the most complex, difficult, and challenging with the potential of being the most rewarding, satisfying, and wonderful game played on the face of this earth. However, like every other game, there are competitive forces at work and there are winners and losers. So for players in the game, the question becomes this: what do you need to do to be victorious?

★★★★★★★★★★★

*Life is a game, the most complex, difficult, and challenging
with the potential of being the most rewarding, satisfying, and
wonderful game
played on the face of the earth.*

★★★★★★★★★★★

If you will allow me to digress back to the game of football, let's look at a few of the similarities between it and the game of life. Often we play with a ball that can take crazy bounces; we are not alone, but in fact are a part of numerous teams; we have different gifts and talents; certainly, there are diverse ways to score points; our plans constantly change to meet various circumstances; we must sometimes play defense; and we need to realize that we are not necessarily the best players on the field.

However, at this point I want to focus mainly on the fact that football has four fifteen-minute quarters with a halftime in the middle. Beyond that, though, each of these quarters has equal designated *playing* time; the *actual* time it takes to play one can vary significantly in the course of the contest. So what does this have to do with the game of life?

One could look at life's progression from many angles, but I believe that it can fall logically into four evolving periods with a break in the middle. It could be equally divided into quarters based on the average life span of an individual, but we all know that each person

8

is unique so the actual time required to complete each quarter will vary. The same types of clock-stopping events that occur in the sport of football can also happen in life. Remember some of them: time-outs, penalties, injuries, being out of bounds, first downs ... lightning strikes, and commercials. We could easily translate any of these into real-life experiences. I am amazed with the similarities that can interrupt the movement of the clock in these two games. Yet there are also differences. For example, the game of football is played in a few hours in the afternoon or evening; the other takes a lifetime and beyond. Also, unfortunately some people are not given an entire life span to complete the game. But, even in those cases, a life can still have purpose and be victorious.

So let's get started. Let's walk together through our life journeys. Let's share with each other experiences in various chapters of our lives. I give it organization by creating a template made up of four quarters and a halftime. Much that you will hear from me, I gained from my own conversations and interactions with others. At the end of each of the following periods, I invite you to do a self-analysis of your game thus far. But probably more importantly, I hope that you will give serious thought to where you are right now regarding your purpose in life. If you are not yet in the fourth quarter, you have some additional time and opportunity to prepare. If you are already there, get excited because, in my Southern vernacular, "God ain't through with you yet!"

What do you think?

"Everyone who competes in the **games** goes into strict training. They do it to get a crown that will not last; but we do it to get a crown that will last forever" (1 Corinthians 9:25).

The Game of Life – Self-Analysis

1. Do you believe that life is a game? If so, why? If not, why?

2. Are there similarities between the game of football and the game of life? If not, is there a better analogy? What is it?

3. Do you think that it is logical to divide life into four quarters? If not, how would you break it down?

4. What about halftime? Does life have one?

5. In life, are there times to play defense as well as offense? When?

6. Is winning in life important like winning in football? Explain.

Chapter 3

THE FIRST QUARTER

SOMETIMES BEGINNINGS CAN BE hard; the initial kick-off of a football game can be nerve-racking. It will remain that way until the ball touches your hands or you make physical contact with an opposing player. Thankfully, you soon fall into a rhythm or pattern that will serve you well during the competition for the ultimate prize. Even at this early stage, winning becomes our objective, though we have an entire game to play. The game has begun.

As we analyze these different periods of the game of life, I realize that it will be very difficult to determine a single purpose for each quarter. However, I want us to attempt to do just that while recognizing multiple interests and desires will be going on concurrently. I believe that if we really focus, a primary purpose—the main thing in our development as a person growing and playing out the game—can be identified for each period.

What is the first quarter? I believe that it begins at birth and ends when one becomes recognized as an adult. Generally, it culminates at the point of independence. In my case, it was when I got my own address. This came after completing college and getting married.

To me personally, purpose in the first quarter is a little more difficult to define. First, it has been so long since I was there, and secondly, many things have changed over the years. To put this in perspective, I can remember making sure the telephone ring was ours because we were on a party line (sharing service with another home) and watching my first television program on a black-and-white TV. What a contrast to iPhones and HD television today. So that I won't appear to be a dinosaur, I am going to rely heavily on my grandchildren and a few others to keep me straight as we venture through this quarter. I hope you don't mind, but I, like every other grandparent, have to brag a little on my grandchildren. Each one of them is so dear to me, but interestingly, they all are living out their purpose in different ways—even in this early phase of life.

When I asked them what their purpose was, they looked at me sort of funny, making me know right off that I needed to approach it differently with them. Thus, after watching and getting a feel for their language and customs, I asked, "What's going on?"

Here is what I observed:

Greta (five) is in kindergarten and already knows how to read, add, and sing on pitch. One day Greta wants to be Gretel in *The Sound of Music*. Though she is our youngest grandchild, she has probably told me more than any of the others, "I love you!"

Nathan (eight) is in first grade (he missed an entire year as he battled cancer and has been in remission for more than four years). He is doing great in school and just recently earned his second-level karate belt. Due to his illness, he has some physical limitations, and in awarding the belt, his instructor made an interesting comment. He stated, "Though Nathan has more reasons than any other to say, 'I can't,' he always says, 'I can!'" He is also an expert on dinosaurs. (Maybe that's why he has such a good relationship with me.)

Noah (nine) is a good student in third grade and a great little athlete (baseball and basketball). I was so proud of him at a recent basketball game; he is a guard and was the leading scorer that day. In the second half, I noticed that he deliberately gave up several easy-scoring opportunities so he could pass the ball to other players. This was the first game of the year when every single player on the team scored. I observed afterward how every one of them was full of enthusiasm and couldn't wait 'til the next game. Noah loves outdoor activities, so he is my special fishing buddy.

Jordan (ten) is in the fifth grade, is in advanced classes, and is a wiz at computers and constructing things. This year he competed for his school in the annual Reading Bowl. He asked me recently to review the animated movie he was making with his digital camera and personal computer. Though I hardly understood anything Jordan was doing with all this technology, he was patient and kind in his explanation.

Alexandria (eleven), also a fifth grader, is a straight-A student, and has some real artistic talents. When she was eight, her great grandmother (my mom), who was ninety at the time, asked her to illustrate a children's book that she had written. This turned out to be a fascinating project that I will share with you later. Elizabeth (great grandmother) recognized and thanked Alexandria often for her artistic contribution to the book. Alexandria sent a birthday card to Elizabeth on her next birthday and wrote, "Grandmama, the words were good too!"

Lindsey (sixteen) is a high school sophomore and an excellent student. She began driving this year, which resulted in an increased prayer life for her parents and for us. She has even shared with me several ways she has attempted to support and help some of her friends; I would want to have a friend like Lindsey. Interestingly, she and I have talked a little about the first quarter. I sensed that she was becoming anxious to finish it strong … go to college and move on into the second quarter. Her belief is the next quarter brings "freedom."

I have also had some serious conversations with those I would call older youth and young adults. I get the feeling from them that, as they approach the first change in quarters, the need to understand, find, and have purpose and meaning becomes more important. From almost all these, regardless of where they are in this quarter, I sensed a need to prepare for whatever comes next. This seems to be a constant, regardless of social or economic status and even maturity and intellect.

From all this, coupled with my empirical knowledge that has begun to return, I have concluded that *learning* is the primary purpose of the first quarter. When I have shared this revelation with others, I have almost unanimously received affirmative headshakes. However, I believe that we need to view learning in a very broad sense. Certainly, learning involves formal education; most everyone residing in this quarter is immersed in that. But it is much more than gaining knowledge. It also includes things like learning to get along, learning from relationships, learning to be responsible, learning who you are, and on and on. I believe another characteristic of this first period is that it is primarily played out while under the direct authority of someone else (e.g., parents, teachers, coaches, and mentors).

★★★★★★★★★★★

... it is primarily played out while under the direct authority of someone else ...

★★★★★★★★★★★

As I share my findings with you, I would be the first to admit that my conversations and observations have been almost exclusively with children, youth, and young adults who are in relatively stable and homogeneous home situations. They have benefited greatly from this, and as a result, they probably are more thoughtful, responsible, and mature than others. At the same time, I realize that many in our society are trapped in dysfunctional and intolerable situations or where priorities and values are distorted. But I continue to conclude that learning is still the purpose, despite the unfortunate fact that some are learning the wrong lessons. This is significant because the first quarter is possibly the most important. It encompasses one's formative years that can establish patterns of behavior for all the quarters that follow.

Again, though the primary purpose of the first quarter is *learning,* keep in mind that it doesn't stop here. Those who are wise learn quickly that this wonderful purpose will continue for a lifetime; just degree and emphasis will change. Please, shake your head up and down in agreement!

Now I want you to do some thinking about your first quarter by answering a few questions.

> "Listen, my sons (and daughters) … pay attention and gain understanding. I give you sound **learning**, so do not forsake my teaching" (Proverbs 4:1–2).

The First Quarter – Self-Analysis

1. What is your definition of the first quarter?

2. Are you still in it? If so, what do you believe is your purpose? If not, did you think about purpose when you were there?

3. Do you think that people today are more or less likely to think about purpose and meaning than their parents?

4. Have you known people who seemed to have purpose in their early years? If so, what were they like?

5. Who and what had the greatest influence on your life during the first quarter?

6. In what way has your first quarter shaped your life?

Chapter 4

THE SECOND QUARTER

THE REFEREE BLOWS THE whistle to end the first quarter and we'll have a minute or two before we move on into the second one. In real life, we may not even recognize the end of the last and the beginning of the next period. When does the second quarter begin, and when will it end? Remember, life like football can vary in the actual length of a quarter, so it will probably be somewhat different for each of us. However, as I indicated earlier, my second quarter began when I completed college, married Snookie, moved into our first apartment, and began work in my chosen field. It lasted almost thirty years and ended when our children were launched and our nest became empty again. In retrospect, I now view this as probably the busiest, most demanding time of my life. During this period leading to the game's halftime, many things were going on, often simultaneously. However, despite the quarter's hectic nature, it was also a wonderful and enjoyable time. In my case, this included a marriage to the very best, raising three special children, and beginning what would become a very fulfilling career.

What is the primary purpose of the second quarter? Here my source for updated information is a group of young friends of ours, plus our own three married children. All of these are in the midst of their second quarters, and I am blessed with the good, open, and honest relationships that we share. Among this group are a lawyer, a doctor, a pastor, a teacher, large and small business leaders, a musician, stay-at-home moms (including a home-teacher), and several other professional types. They all have different stories to tell, so the main challenge is to find some common traits that will lead us to the answer to that important question: what is your purpose right now in the second quarter?

The first thing that I rediscovered is that this quarter carries with it a tremendous *burden of responsibility*. Many decisions that will be made carry lasting effects and will shape our lives for the long term. Our minds are full of more questions than answers. How am I going to support myself? Who am I going to spend my life with? Where am I going to live? How am I going to handle this new freedom that comes with adulthood? What kind of family will I have? Up to this point, family was viewed primarily as parents and siblings; now, in most cases, it becomes spouse and children.

I've got to start making a living. I need a job to support myself and ultimately my family. The financial burdens of daily life become real for the first time. Some may have had jobs while still in school and this gave them a head start. But now the temptation of credit and immediate gratification is constant and enticing. The economy may be down, which causes jobs and opportunities to be scarce; hard decisions and changing courses could become necessary. *I may need to go back to school and get another degree or go into a new field. This life may or may not turn out like I planned.* These are some of the financial concerns, but other basic activities during this stage can also weigh heavily upon us. Something minor, coupled with everything else, can become major.

★★★★★★★★★★

... the temptation of credit and immediate gratification is constant and enticing ...

★★★★★★★★★★

Let me give you a humorous example of a minor to major experience. In talking to a stay-at-home mom whose four children had finally reached school age, Diane shared, "I feel so guilty because I have some free time for myself." Snookie told her to enjoy it while it lasted and assured her that this would quickly pass as new and more demands would surely follow. And they did. But, again, the point is that this time can be very burdensome.

Another common characteristic of those in this second quarter is a *thirst for identity.* That's a fancy way of asking, "Who am I now?" Most of them had completed

23

their formal education, so this question sought an answer to a deeper concern. Even though in most cases, their professional, vocational, and home status were becoming well established, there seemed to be a common desire for more in their lives. I remember studying Maslow's hierarchy of needs. It theorizes that, as basic and moderate needs are fulfilled, one's concerns tend to rise to a higher level to gain personal satisfaction. I noticed this in many ways in both large and small matters. An example of this is my son, Jeff. He recently asked my opinion on how he could become more involved in community activities. In addition to this desire, he also agreed to coach his nine-year-old son's basketball team this year. He travels a great deal in his job as a consultant and is highly successful, but I could sense a need on his part for more—in this case, an opportunity to serve beyond his job.

The list of descriptive terms for the second quarter is large; therefore, it can be difficult to attach broad labels. However, I have one additional general statement about the inhabitants of this quarter. They *tend to be bold* in their thinking and actions. When one completes the first quarter, the education that has been attained is largely theoretical. But entry into the second quarter seems to bring an immediate desire to put some of the theories into practice. I sense an entrepreneurial spirit not only in the ones entering the business world but also among those in other fields of endeavor. I personally remember my desire to try, outweighing my fear to fail at that point. Later, I became more conservative in my decision-making as experience taught me the consequences of my actions. I now look back and am a bit sad that my zeal for a new frontier has subsided somewhat. However, I hope that I still remember this lesson: To try is not a failure; failure to try is.

Like the first one, my sources for evaluating the second quarter have largely been those with traditional upbringing and values. However, I believe the inclusion of more untraditional individuals would not have changed the basic conclusion when defining the purpose of the second quarter.

In order to define the purpose of the second quarter, let's review the general characteristics that I discovered in my research. The quarter carries a tremendous *burden of responsibility*; while in it there is a *thirst for identity*; and those there *tend to be bold*. After giving this much thought, I would submit that the purpose of the second quarter is *earning*. In defining it this way, you must consider earning in a broad sense also. In addition to earning your living, you earn your wings and stripes and your place and way. You also seek to earn respect and acceptance during this quarter.

Let's review. The purpose of the first quarter is *learning* and the purpose of the second quarter is *earning*.

Okay! You have reached halftime and glanced at the scoreboard. Take a few minutes and answer the questions below to gain a better understanding of where you stand on some of the issues you've faced. Then you can retreat to the locker room. I'll meet you there.

"Such people we command and urge in the Lord Jesus Christ to settle down and **earn** the bread they eat. And as for you ... never tire of doing what is right" (2 Thessalonians 3:11–13).

The Second Quarter – Self-Analysis

1. In your opinion, when does the second quarter in the game of life start and finish?

2. Was it difficult to move from the first to the second quarter? If so, what were some of the reasons?

3. Was the second quarter burdensome? Was there an identity need and greater tendency toward boldness for those in this period?

4. Do you agree or disagree that *earning* (broad definition) describes the purpose of the second quarter?

5. Who and what had the greatest influence on your life during the second quarter?

6. In what way has this quarter shaped your life?

Chapter 5

HALFTIME

HALFTIME FOR THE FOOTBALL team in the locker room can be brutal or encouraging, but more than likely it is somewhere in between. The first half is behind us, and the second lies ahead. The atmosphere is probably influenced most by the outcome of the first half. Some may think that this is a time to rest and relax, but that can be the farthest from the true purpose and function of this break.

If the first half has gone relatively well, the focus will probably be on the continuation of the successful game plan with a few tweaks here and there. The plays that worked well on offense will be identified and probably used again. The defensive alignments will be reviewed, and the effectiveness in various situations will be noted.

However, if the team is way behind, then a reevaluation of some or all areas of the game plan will quickly point out the need for changes. The most dreaded response during halftime is the wrath of the coach brought on by something called "lack of effort!" A coach can accept being behind to a team with more talent or because of superior coaching of the other team, or even bad luck caused by the bounce of the ball. However, I have never known a coach who will tolerate his players giving less than their best effort. Attitude and commitment are probably the most important aspects of playing the game successfully.

In the game of life, the halftime break can be an exceedingly revealing and crucial time. The term we use to describe this particular point is "midlife." And midlife is hardly ever mentioned without the word "crisis." Midlife crisis has almost become a medical diagnosis in our society. Nearly everyone suffers from this malady to some extent, particularly those of the male gender. What causes this unusual deviation from normal behavior? Below is my conclusion, based on my research and own experience.

★★★★★★★★★★★

... midlife is hardly ever mentioned without the word "crisis."

★★★★★★★★★★★

The first two quarters could have gone one of three ways. First, you could have been crushed by the opponent and feel hopelessly behind; second, you may have performed brilliantly or the opponent was weak and you are comfortably ahead; or third, you are somewhere between these two extremes. I share this with you because I believe that the causes of midlife crises are the result of the outcome of the first two quarters.

Here is my theory: if you had a bad first half, you resist going back out on the field for the second half. It's like so many other things; you don't want to have a repeat bad performance. Conversely, if you had a very good first half, there is an inherent desire to remain there and glow in its success. I believe that one of these two extremes generally is the root cause of serious midlife crises. The basic symptom of this "disease" is immaturity and the unwillingness to go on with your life. Entry into the second half requires you to change your lifestyle and purpose and grow up.

If you suffer from this problem, the good news is that a midlife crisis eventually subsides, hopefully, without too many permanent consequences; and the sooner the better. Then at that point, you can trot back out on the field with your head held high and approach the second half of your life with vigor and enthusiasm. And, as my old Southern coach would say, "Let's go get 'em!"

But first, what do you think?

> "We all, like sheep, have gone astray
> [especially at midlife]" (Isaiah 53:6).

Halftime – Self-Analysis

1. When you reached halftime, did you have a midlife crisis? If so, how severe was it? If not, how did you avoid it?

2. At the end of the first half, did you feel like you were behind or ahead? Explain.

3. Do you agree that the reasons cited are the primary causes of midlife crises? Are there some other reasons also? If so, what are some of them?

4. Who and what had the most impact on your life during your half-time period?

5. Did anything happen during halftime that helped shape your life?

6. If you were asked to define the purpose for halftime in one word, what would it be?

Chapter 6

THE THIRD QUARTER

THERE ARE TWO THINGS that you notice when you start the third quarter: first, if you kicked off at the beginning of the game, you now will receive the ball (or vice versa), and second, you are now facing the opposite end zone. I guess this is an attempt to level the playing field and ensure fairness. It may be a little confusing and require some reorientation at first, but soon you are back into the swing of the game.

Let's give some definition to the third quarter that we are now entering. For me, it started just where we left off at the end of the first half: Snookie and I were new empty nesters and in our early fifties. At the time, we did not realize that this initial second-half period would ultimately be our shortest quarter. The playing clock would keep moving with fewer interruptions like time-outs, injuries, being out of bounds ... lightning strikes, and commercials. It seems that my recollections of this quarter are much clearer than the first two; it hasn't been that long since we were there. Still, it helps to consult with friends and relatives who are currently living out their third quarters as a reminder. For us, this period would last for about fourteen years and was completed when my professional career came to a close.

I have heard coaches and sports commentators emphasize how significant the third quarter is to the outcome of the game. They say that it is crucial to come out strong, create momentum, and establish dominance. If you are on defense, it means stopping the other team's initial drive. If you received the kick and are on offense, your team needs to sustain a drive for an early score. I sense that a concentrated effort at this particular time is a necessity because, even with another quarter to go, you can begin to see the end of the game approaching.

★★★★★★★★★★★

I sense that a concentrated effort at this particular time is a necessity because, even with another quarter to go, you can begin to see the end of the game approaching.

★★★★★★★★★★★

Let's get back to the game of life and attempt to answer an all-important question: What is the purpose of the third quarter? In trying to analyze this period, a review of the two previous quarters might be helpful. Remember, the purpose of the first quarter was *learning* and the second was *earning*. In general, I thought of my formal education time (learning) as being an introduction to many theoretical ideas. Earning, on the other hand, was largely focused on putting ideas to work and thus more practical in nature. Therefore, in the third quarter we *benefit from exposure to both the theoretical and the practical.* Certainly this is helpful as we play out the balance of the game.

No doubt there are exceptions, but I also believe that this is *a time of peaks.* Mentally, physically, and emotionally, I probably was on top of my game. In the few areas that may have declined, I had the ability to compensate. In my profession, I remember headhunters seeking out prospects who were in their early third quarters for the top jobs. In looking back, peaks in my professional, personal, and even spiritual life manifested themselves during this period.

In observing individuals in the midst of third quarter activities, I often saw *a higher level of maturity* not previously obvious. In many cases, relationships have become much deeper and more meaningful, and priorities change. I realize in making this assertion that you can probably cite many contradictions. However, the potential and ability for an individual to maturely play the game and be highly successful has probably never been greater than during this third quarter.

So from all this, what is the purpose of the third quarter? I submit that it is *discerning.* Discerning is defined as keenness, insightfulness, and practical judgment. It is a period in which theory and practice come together. When you peak in many ways and have a high level of maturity, you can, in my opinion, be described as discerning.

The whistle blows; the third quarter has ended. We are really tired after playing three demanding quarters of the game. We take off our helmets, drink a little water from a bottle, and, before moving on, take a brief look back from where we've come. We've spent the first quarter focused on *learning*, second on *earning*, passed through our *midlife* break, and just completed the third: *discerning*. Can you believe it?

We have one more quarter to play! Your turn!

"The wise in heart are called discerning"
(Proverbs 13:19).

The Third Quarter – Self-Analysis

1. In your opinion, when does the third quarter of the game of life start and finish?

2. Was it difficult to get back into the game after reaching midlife?

3. Did your first two quarters help prepare you for the second half? In what ways?

4. Did you feel that you were at the top of your game in the third quarter? Explain.

5. Do you think that discernment is an accurate way to describe purpose in the third quarter?

6. In what way has the third quarter shaped your life?

Chapter 7

THE FOURTH QUARTER

YOU MAY HAVE ATTENDED a football game or watched one on television and noticed a strange occurrence toward the middle of the second half. On both sidelines, you observe all the players holding up four fingers. What is happening? It is the beginning of the fourth and final period of the game, and this is each team's way of expressing commitment to finish strong and victoriously. You even get excited because you too feel something special is occurring. You cannot help sensing a renewed enthusiasm and energy among them, despite the fact that they have already played for three demanding quarters. Certainly, each quarter has its significance, but when the final whistle is blown at the end of the fourth one, we all know the game is over and the score is final. Should the game of life be approached in a similar manner? You betcha! So let's begin!

Before starting, I do not want to minimize the obvious feeling of uncertainty that can accompany this particular period. Health and financial issues often rise to the top. In my case, the gait in my walk is progressively slowing each year, and I have been relegated to "follower" in my daily three–mile walk with Snookie. I pray that I won't outlive my mind. Also, will our resources be adequate so we will not be a burden on others? These two factors in particular (health and wealth) can weigh heavily. But for now, let's be positive.

★★★★★★★★★★★

These two factors in particular
(health and wealth) can weigh heavily.

★★★★★★★★★★★

Like the first three, I would like to start by defining the fourth quarter, including when it begins and when it ends. My review and analysis of the first three quarters have not been that difficult for me for two reasons. First, I had a lot of help from those currently residing in each of these, and secondly, I personally have completed all three. However, this one is much tougher for me. I have no problem determining when it began. I raised my four fingers into the air when I left my job after forty years and joined the ranks of the "retired." I learned quickly that this is probably the most recognized group in our society. On just about every form, there is a place to check "retired." We tend to be profiled as the oldies and even have national associations vying for our membership. Social Security and Medicare became a common addition to our vocabulary.

Such things made it easy for me to define the beginning of my final quarter. But let me quickly add that other individuals may retire much earlier or later than I, so they may claim a different fourth quarter starting point. However, my problem is not the beginning but the end. I have observed that the fourth quarter in some cases is the shortest and in others it is the longest in this game called life. The game delayers seem to be more prevalent here than anywhere else. I will need to draw from a much broader group to help me better understand the complexities and challenges of this very different quarter and, most importantly, to define its purpose. For the time being, please allow me to defer defining the end of the fourth quarter until later. However, I would offer this observation: it's over when it's over.

One of my early duties in the fourth quarter was to grocery shop. After a few training sessions, Snookie sent me alone to pick up a few items at our Kroger grocery store. By chance, this first excursion was on seniors day; I recognized this immediately because so many older folks were in the store and some buses from the local assisted living centers were in the parking lot. When I arrived at the cashier to check out, I inquired about the senior discount. Without hesitation, she replied, "I need to see your driver's license to make sure you qualify."

At that, I pulled it out and showed it to her with pride, since I was evidently youthful looking enough to require age verification. However, this gloating was short lived, for behind me in line was a nice lady in her late eighties who was in one of those scooter carts. Before she could place all her groceries on the conveyor belt, the cashier said, "I will need to see your identification to make sure you qualify for the senior discount." As I was leaving, she looked at me, smiled, and then winked. I learned at that very moment that all of us in the fourth quarter have something in common. We need to have a sense of humor even as we covet the respect of others and a definition of our purpose.

For some reason, purpose seems to be harder to get your arms around in this quarter. During the time that I was working on this particular chapter, I read one of my favorite author's columns in the local newspaper. It was pertinent to this subject. Here's what Dear Abby offered:

> I am a 64-year-old healthy widow ... I retired a year ago after a successful 42-year career. I am financially sound. I couldn't wait to retire because my job was demanding, and toward the end, it had become extremely stressful. About two months into retirement—and after taking a few trips—I began feeling worthless and guilty for being nonproductive. I tried a part-time job, but it wasn't my thing ... I feel like I lost my identity when I stopped working ... want to engage in some activity that will revive my self-worth. At this point, I don't know what that will be ... SEARCHING FOR "ME."

I have found this request for guidance to be common among many entering this final period. Interestingly, Abby responded,

> When people tell me they are thinking of retiring, I always ask, "And what will you be retiring TO? Because I am convinced that retiring to "nothing" is neither physically nor emotionally healthy for individuals who are used to being active.[2]

Great advice!

A common response that I receive when querying fourth-quarterers is this: "I want to leave something for the next generation." There seems to be a desire to share something of value that one has accumulated, pass on an inheritance, and establish a legacy. We sometimes think of material wealth in this context, but I sense that it is much more than this with most folks. Actually, I believe that things like respect, integrity, values, service, caring attitudes, and just basic wisdom are among the attributes most want identified when their names are called. To be honest, I feel this way too.

I can cite many more similar examples of struggles, challenges, and needs experienced by those making the transition from the third to the four quarter as the end of the game approaches. So, what *is* the purpose of this final quarter? From all of this, I have concluded that the best term describing the purpose of the fourth quarter is *yearning*. In this context, yearning means wanting, longing, craving, or deeply desiring something. This "something" might be correcting a wrong, experiencing a right, continuing a joy, or gracefully passing the baton to those who follow. In summary, I believe these fourth-quarter dwellers *yearn for a strong finish and victory* in the great game of life.

I have a friend who refuses to be recognized as a retiree; he vigorously describes himself as a *re-firee!* I actually have added that term to my own resume. Some specific examples might be helpful to further emphasize the importance of purpose in the fourth quarter.

Fourth-Quarter Experiences

Often when an author gets personal, he/she will issue a disclaimer or will qualify something that is about to be shared. However, instead of a disclaimer, I am issuing a "claimer." In other words, I claim the following to be significant happenings that have had eternal influence on my life. The first almost cost me my life but instead changed it dramatically.

Grand Entry into Retirement

Approximately two months before my retirement that would move me into the fourth quarter, I was already in the post-career mode. At home, I was doing projects that I had put off too long. One of these was a large, dead, pine tree in our side yard next to the dog pen that needed to come down. Though I had some experience in this area, this particular tree was a little tricky because it needed to fall back into the woods. To complicate things further, it was among other trees which might impede it from going down in the right direction. So I did the prudent thing: I tied it to another tree to assure the correct trajectory of the fall. I learned later my mistake was that dead trees are very unpredictable. The fall started in the right direction, but when it met resistance from the other trees it broke off and began to come down the opposite way. I tried my best to escape and at least had the presence of mind to throw the chain saw to the side as I ran.

But, the bulk of the trunk hit me directly. After I felt the impact on my upper back and right shoulder, I lay on the ground for about twenty minutes, trying not to go into shock. It took that long before I could muster the strength to get into the house. It's interesting what goes through your mind at times of crisis. I remember thinking, *I am going to die just a couple of months before I retire; Snookie will probably remarry and her next husband will enjoy the fruits of all my hard work and labor.* It sounds funny now, but it was very serious then.

Snookie, however, was my hero in this experience. She kept her cool, which helped me keep mine. She did not once scold me for my poor judgment—that came later when she decreed prohibitions on some of my handyman activities. I was in the hospital overnight with a fractured scapular (I later learned how unusual it is to break this strongest bone in the body) and cracked ribs. Both the ER physician and orthopedist indicated in a very serious manner that if the tree had hit me just four inches to the left, I would be either dead or paralyzed. Fortunately, today I experience very few physical repercussions from all this.

However, the spiritual effect has been significant. Though I am not usually a "what if" person, this episode really caused me to reflect and ask instead "what now?" My conclusion is that God had something else in mind for me after my professional career ended. I was looking forward to other projects, traveling, golfing, fishing, hunting, etc., but none of these in themselves seemed to offer fulfillment and meaning to this new phase of life that I was entering. I truly believe that something more was needed and expected, and God had spared me for a special reason. I was almost fully recovered when I officially retired, so I raised my four fingers in the air with renewed excitement and also thanksgiving as I began my fourth quarter.

As a result of all this, I embarked on a new career. I initially called it "purposeful retirement" and then "refiring," and it has been just as fulfilling as my previous careers. In addition to a few recreational endeavors, it has included volunteering, teaching, mentoring, speaking, consulting, and writing.

The Two-Minute Warning

As I mentioned earlier, professional football is my least favorite level of the sport. However, it has a unique rule that brings unusual excitement and drama to the game that doesn't exist at the amateur level. Time is called when the game clock reaches two minutes prior to the end of the game; this alerts both teams that it will soon be over. But more importantly, these last two minutes, if managed well, can produce an exciting climax to the event. Both teams give it their all in an attempt to either come from behind or maintain their lead. Back to my analogy. I'm not certain that the two-minute warning applies in every case in life's game; however, I have no doubt that there are occasions that it does. Let me share one with you.

For my mother's ninetieth birthday, we were at a loss in selecting an appropriate gift. After a great deal of thought, one of my sisters suggested that we publish one of Mom's little children's poems. She had always wanted to have some of her writings published and had succeeded only once with a short story (a couple of paragraphs) in *Reader's Digest*. We found one that she had recently written called "Who I'd Like to Be." We made arrangements with a publisher to have 250 copies printed for family members and friends. When Mom opened the letter from the publisher requesting permission to publish the little book, she was excited and immediately expressed her desire that it be illustrated by one of her great grandchildren.

Alexandria Elizabeth Brown, who has artistic talent and incidentally is named for her great grandmother Elizabeth, was selected and enthusiastically accepted the challenge. The project took a few months to complete. The little book that is about a boy who wondered what it would be like to be something else—a bird, a bee, a duck, a frog, a pig, a turtle—was a hit with everyone.

Mom was delighted and proud of this special gift, and it was a blessing to us all. Though she was still relatively active then, I believe this project gave her a renewed sense of purpose. That would have been enough, but it didn't end there.

Mom gave a copy to a friend who was acquainted with the first lady of our state (Georgia). Our governor's wife, Mrs. Sandra Deal, a retired schoolteacher, borrowed and began reading the little book to pre-K and kindergarten students throughout the state to promote reading and literacy. It was so popular with the children that Mrs. Deal wanted copies to leave with them—many of whom had never had a book of their own. Through a series of events, a second printing supported by a grant was initiated, and now thousands of these little books are making their way to students, schools, and libraries. And others are being sold with proceeds going to a ministry that supports families with children with cancer. I spend many days carrying books to Mom's nursing home room for her to sign. Each time she scribbles "Elizabeth" on a page, a child is about to be blessed.

One day after one of our autograph sessions, I decided to get Mom's thoughts about this project in which I was involved. I didn't know what she would say and even if she would understand my questions. Since her book was published, she has suffered from a series of falls and dementia that is increasing. She is now ninety-three. I share with you our conversation that I took pains to record verbatim.

Bernie: Mom, I need for you to help me with something. I'm working on a project called *Purpose in the Fourth Quarter.* Since both you and I are in this last quarter of our lives, you might have some good ideas.

Mom: I don't like the way you said that. This needs to be given serious thinking, but when explaining it you need to keep it simple and understandable.

Bernie: I agree, but Mom, what do you think your purpose is now?

Mom: To leave something for those who come after us!

Bernie: Do you mean something specific or sharing with them some of the lessons you have learned?

Mom: Yes! That's right. If someone asks me something, I might can help because 'I've been there, done that' in some cases.

Bernie: What specifically can you do now?

Mom: I've had to reconsider some things. You know that there are things that I used to do that I can't do anymore, but there are some things that I still can do.

Bernie: So …

Mom: My purpose is to continue to do those things that I can do the best I can.

Bernie: Does being a Christian have anything to do with your purpose?

Mom: Of course. You must act, talk, and live as much like Christ as possible!

Bernie: But Mom, what specifically can you do now?

Mom: *I can still love and encourage others for the glory of God!*

Bernie: (It took a minute for me to respond.) I can think of no higher purpose. Thanks, Mom. You not only helped me with my project, but you also helped me with my own life. I just hope and pray that I can have such special purpose in my fourth quarter.

A short time later, I witnessed Mom still doing what she can do. She was in the corner of her room in her recliner, and I was trying to engage her in conversation. Behind us, I heard a noise, turned around, and watched as a lady in a wheelchair entered the room. My salutation drew no clear response as she guided the chair with her feet closer and closer to Mom. I was a bit concerned until Mom said, "This is my neighbor. I help her sometime." (They can't remember each other's name.) Then something very unusual happened. The woman raised one foot and put it up on Mom's chair. Because Mom was leaning back in a reclined position, she glanced over and asked me, "Bernie, could you tie her shoe? It came undone." I tied it for her, and she lowered her leg and walked her wheelchair out of the room. Only gibberish sounds were uttered by the lady, but my mom knew exactly what she needed. I observed in amazement and was blessed!

I can add no more. My mom is running up the score after the two-minute warning in the fourth quarter.

As I mentioned earlier, the fourth quarter can be very difficult; I often hear, "Getting old is not for sissies." Having worked for over forty years in the health-care field, I have observed firsthand the effects of the aging process both physically and mentally. But I have been inspired by many who, despite enormous limitations, still maintain a sense of purpose. Regardless of the obstacles, the fourth quarter can be a very special one because it benefits from the experiences and wisdom gained in the first three. To turn its purpose (yearning), no matter how small, into reality is the measure of success. As my mom said, "My purpose is to continue to do those things that I can do the best I can."

Overtime – Sudden Life

As I was writing this, I was constantly exchanging thoughts with others, and as a result many new ideas kept emerging. Usually I would add a sentence or two that might capture the essence of a particular thought. However, one theme kept arising that I believe needs some additional conversation. This came to a head when my insurance agent, an avid football fan, said, "What about the fifth quarter—overtime?" Even though I had mentioned this casually, Wilson convinced me that a more in-depth look was needed.

It's interesting that in the various levels of football, different methods are used to determine a winner when the game ends in a tie. In my view, the most dramatic and decisive is at the professional level—the first team that scores in the overtime period is the winner. They call it "sudden death!"

In the game of life, I believe that more folks than we realize find themselves tied at the end of regulation and therefore go into overtime. The final outcome of their game has not been determined. I remember attending the funeral of a neighbor several years ago. He was a highly successful engineer, a great husband and family man, and a good friend. His daughter's husband, in delivering the eulogy, told of his father-in-law's last days in the hospital. His wife, a strong, committed Christian, was not sure that her husband was saved and could not imagine him not being with her in heaven. Through persistence and an unwillingness to take a chance, his wife, son-in-law, and family members shared the good news of salvation with their loved one. Though Ed had heard it many times, for the first time he truly understood and believed. (It was not by coincidence that acquaintances around the world were also praying for his salvation.) His funeral was one of the greatest worship services that I have ever attended. In overtime, he received "sudden life!" [3]

I realize that I still have not specifically addressed this question: when does the fourth quarter end? That is so intriguing to me that I want to spend some more time on just this subject in the final chapters. But let's review the purposes thus far: The purpose of the first quarter is *learning;* the second is *earning;* the third is *discerning,* and the fourth is *yearning.* Now, have your say!

"A longing (**yearning**) fulfilled is sweet to the soul"
(Proverbs 13:19).

The Fourth Quarter – Self-Analysis

1. In your opinion, when does the fourth quarter of life begin?

2. Is there any excitement when it begins? Or is there a letdown? Explain.

3. Can you usually identify persons in the fourth quarter? Are there signs other than appearance?

4. Do you like the word retired? If so, why? If not, why?

5. What makes the fourth quarter different from the first three? Explain.

6. Has someone who is residing after the two-minute warning in the fourth quarter inspired you? Share.

7. How about overtime—sudden life? Share.

8. What is the purpose of the fourth quarter in your mind?

Chapter 8

THE PURPOSE OF THE GAME OF LIFE

IN ORDER TO KNOW our purpose in life, we must first know the Creator of life. So I begin with an experience that was helpful to me in understanding my connection with the Creator. I want to share with you something one of my friends told our small group at a recent Sunday school retreat.

Before retirement, he worked for many years with the Federal Reserve and was deeply involved in transactional activities between it and banks throughout the country. *Billions* of dollars were being handled daily, and the infrastructure and systems were crucial to the well-being of the financial system of the entire country. Continuous connectivity was essential. In a somewhat matter-of-fact yet serious tone, he said, "I can't tell you how good it felt each morning when I arrived at work to see that the mainframe was running!" He reflected on the few times something had gone wrong and the chaos, confusion, and utter disruption that resulted despite many backup measures.

Sid was not thinking about the wonderful spiritual metaphor he was making while sharing just a daily requirement that made things work. Discovering and fulfilling our *purpose* can only happen if we are connected to the mainframe and "the mainframe is running." The good news is that the spiritual mainframe is always running. God is so great that He never has to shut down for preventive maintenance and so good that He can handle an infinite number of transactions simultaneously. If we are struggling with things like finding meaning in our life, we don't need to Google; we just need to pray. So let's share our thoughts on the real *purpose of the game of life*.

★★★★★★★★★★★

… we don't need to Google; we just need to pray.

★★★★★★★★★★★

Over the years, the life cycle we humans experience has been portrayed in many forms. It has been compared to a race, a journey, even a battle, and it also has been likened to the seasons of the year. I have chosen to compare it to a game, specifically football. Regardless of the choice of analogies, I believe that life is a progression that leads somewhere, and at its core there is purpose.

In a football game, each quarter has its unique characteristics and focus, but in the end the goal never changes. The purpose of the effort is to win the game. I contend that similar dynamics are in play in the game of life. Even though each quarter has a distinct purpose, there is still an overall purpose that guides us to victorious living. We have individually examined each quarter of the game to determine its focus. And I realize that the various quarterly purposes that I have identified are not exclusive. To some degree, you can find all those purposes in every quarter. I also might add that some have disagreed with me on some of these and their sequence. For example, one person suggested that the second quarter is yearning instead of earning, third is earning instead of discerning, and fourth is discerning substituted for yearning; and I concede that for him that may have been the case. But in general, I stick by my choices and sequence.

While debating this is an interesting intellectual exercise, I believe that it's much more important that we not lose sight of the game's overall purpose. As I attempt to approach this subject, *the purpose of the game of life*, I feel more than intimidated; I feel inadequate and almost illiterate. So why would a plain, old, Southern, sort of redneck, *refiree* want to venture into this territory where even the great theologians and philosophers tread with some degree of trepidation? There are probably many reasons, but the main one is that I have a deep and burning desire to know just *why I'm here (my purpose) and what I need to do to win this great game of life.*

I have been a Christian almost all my life, so I have been taught that I was created by God and He has a purpose for me. Dr. Kathy Koch put it this way: "You were created on purpose with a purpose."[4] But what is it and how can I be sure that I am on the right track? Not being a Bible scholar, I probably won't put all this in just the right words, but I will try to share some of the lessons and principles that I have gained during my journey in our effort to discover the true purpose of life. My dad, in his sermons, always had three points. He would say, "That's about all folks can absorb in one sitting." So I'm going to try to express myself using his model.

Three of my favorite Bible Scriptures are John 3:16, Romans 8:28, and Matthew 22:36–40. I believe each of these will assist in solving the riddle of life's purpose. They have been helpful to me. I will share my three thoughts.

First, we need to be loved and not lost.

So many of us are lost; we are living our lives aimlessly and often recklessly. The message that I hear constantly is "Do your own thing. You only have one life to live; just do it." So as the old Frank Sinatra song suggests, "I Did It My Way." Certainly, it is important to be self-assured with good self-esteem, but I have learned over the years that wisdom is the realization of how little, rather than how much, I know. I truly believe that we all are to an extent lost. You cannot be saved until you know you are lost, and so many times we may not even realize how lost we really are.

Interestingly, I have found that when I feel loved, I cease to feel lost. Therefore, it is essential that we know that we are loved. I observed this in a vivid way recently when a young friend of ours (in the second quarter with three children) lost her husband after a valiant battle with cancer. Part of her died in a very real sense, and I'm certain that she felt hopelessly lost. Over the next months, now almost a year, God, through the use of her family and many friends, "loved her back to life." Though the grief has not totally subsided and the void will probably never be totally filled, we can see a return to purpose in her life. While being lost promotes purposelessness, being loved promotes purposefulness. Love is the road map that can lead us out of the swamp of meaninglessness. We need to be loved, not lost.

> "For God so loved the world that He gave
> His only Son, that whoever believes in
> Him shall not perish but have eternal life"
> (John 3:16).

Second, we need to be called, not cursed.

To be honest, I have struggled with my *calling*. Over the years, I had heard so many Christians share their testimonies that often portrayed a dramatic tale of spiritual rags to riches. I envied them and in a spiritual way felt short-changed or cursed because I did not have such a story to tell, even though I considered myself a good churchman and a committed Christian. And unfortunately, there were times due to egotism that I even thought that God should be honored to have me on His team.

But, for some reason, you sort of know when your life and His call are not aligned. I particularly struggled with this in my professional career. When I arrived at my professional pinnacle (CEO of a large health-care organization), I felt an emptiness and lack of fulfillment that should not accompany such achievement. What do you do if your career path and your faith journey seem to be out of sync, particularly if you are in a leadership role? In an odd sense, my success became a curse—why should I be unhappy with such earthly accomplishments? (You may think that *curse* is too strong of a word, but I don't.) I seriously began to wonder if I had answered the wrong call. Then my pastor and dear friend, in one of his best sermons delivered at just the right time, gave me help and clarity. He said, "Your calling may not be to do something different, but instead it may be to do what you are doing differently." That intensified my quest to learn how to do my job differently by seeking guidance from the One who has the answers. We need to be called, not cursed.

> "And we know that in all things God
> works for the good of those who love
> Him, who have been called according to
> His purpose"
> (Romans 8:28).

And third, we need to love, not leave.

I once had a very good friend who just wrote people off. What I mean by this is that when there was a disagreement or conflict in a relationship, he just abandoned or left it, many times without even realizing what he was doing. He had been my friend for many years and our wives were very close. So I worked hard to make sure I didn't do something that would cause him to write me off. I'll be honest that I was uncomfortable with this relationship because of its fragile nature. Chris Pine, reflecting on his role in the recent movie *People Like Us,* identified the same issue when he said, "They (family and acquaintances) are not superhuman. They are real, screwed-up, faulted people. The only thing you have a choice over is if you choose to accept and love them, or push them out of your life and resent them."[5]

Though my friend would probably never admit it, I sense real emptiness and loneliness in his life. I believe that he has the ability to love, but it is conditional. Unfortunately, from time to time, I believe we all have a bit of "write-off" tendencies in our own spiritual DNA. My role model for the attribute called unconditional love is my dad, who died over twenty years ago. He was a pastor who loved and was loved by more folks than anyone I have ever known. At his death, one of his pastor colleagues told me, "I have never known anyone who loved to love people more than your dad!" That was his legacy; I hope that I caught this disease called *love* from him. We need to love not leave.

> "Which is the greatest commandment in the law? Jesus replied: 'Love the Lord your God with all your heart and with all your soul and with all your mind.' This is the first and greatest commandment. And the second is like it: 'Love your neighbor as yourself'"
> (Matthew 22:36–39).

I believe that these three Scriptures and many others support the same theme in capturing the essence of life's purpose from a Christian perspective. We first need to be loved (and know it), we need to be called (and answer it), and finally, we need to love (and give it). If any of these are missing in your life, my advice to you is the same that was given to me. Do it!

There have been many helpful books written on "purpose," but my all-time favorite is Rick Warren's *The Purpose Driven Life.* Several of his points are particularly provocative and inspiring to me. For example, "You won't discover your life's meaning by looking within yourself ... Life is about letting God use you for His purposes, not your using Him for your own purposes ... Being successful and fulfilling your life's purpose are not at all the same issue!"[6]

To these and so many more statements in that wonderful, life-changing book, I say amen!

I would like to share one other experience that has been helpful to me in defining purpose. Hopefully, this will also be meaningful to you.

Several years ago, I became involved in a series of leadership conferences called Bridging the Gap. These mainly dealt with the gap that often exists between one's career path and faith journey. In various venues, speakers were invited to share "bridging the gap" experiences in their individual worlds. A doctor spoke on bridging the gap in the operating room; a CEO in the business world; a coach in the sports arena; a restaurateur in the kitchen; a musician on the stage; a politician on the hill; a homemaker in the home; a Miss America in the limelight; and probably the most inspiring was a young, collegiate baseball player who had been injured and was paralyzed. He spoke on "Changing my platform from a baseball diamond to a wheelchair."

What enlightening testimonies all of these were as individuals shared spiritual journeys in different settings. In conjunction with these programs, Snookie and I wrote a poem that ultimately was put to music as a theme song. It seems appropriate here, because it was our effort to share our heart-felt need to connect with God as we journey together. As you might expect, we titled it "Bridging the Gap."

Bridging the Gap

1. There is a gap 'tween God and me.
   Must bridge that gap so I can be
   Someone who finds that long lost key.
   Please, God, come down and set me free.

2. I live a life that's all 'bout me;
   The world says take, and I agree.
   Fortune and fame are what I seek,
   Yet peace and joy I cannot keep.

3. The Word came down, said, "Follow me."
   I did just that, now I can see.
   He gave His life on a rugged tree;
   I met Him there at Calvary.

4. We bridged that gap 'tween God and me;
   And praise to Him, I now can be
   One who has found that long-lost key.
   He rose again and set me free![7]

So let's sum it all up by answering the sixty-four-thousand-dollar question. What is the purpose of the game of life? But first, a review of the purposes of the individual quarters: first is *learning*; second is *earning*; third is *discerning,* and fourth is *yearning*. Though each has its unique focus, I believe that the overall purpose of life is constant and exists in each of these quarters.

The answer: ***The purpose of life is to love God, your neighbor, and yourself, and to receive and respond to God's love and call.***

If this is your purpose, I am confident that God will give you the gifts, graces, and fruits needed to live a victorious life. This is my view. Now let me have yours.

"Many are the plans in a man's heart, but it
is the Lord's **purpose** that prevails"
(Proverbs 19:21).

The Purpose of the Game of Life – Self-Analysis

1. Do you agree or disagree with the quarterly purposes and their sequence as described in the preceding chapter? If not, what would yours be?

2. Have you ever considered that your life has an overall purpose?

3. Do you consider yourself a Christian? If so, how does your faith relate to your purpose?

4. Are you loved? By whom? Do you feel called? By whom? Do you love? Whom?

5. Is there a gap between God and you? If so, how can it be bridged?

6. What is the purpose of your life?

Chapter 9

WINNING: THE REPLAY

LET'S DIGRESS A MOMENT. In chapter one, we determined the objective of a football game is winning, and I contended that the goal of the game of life is also winning. So let's talk about winning and what it means. In football, it is obvious which team wins—it's the one with the highest score. Even if the game is tied at the end of regulation and goes into overtime, ultimately there will be a winner. I asked earlier if you think that God cares who wins on the football field. Most folks I have asked say, "No!" But I respectfully disagree; I believe that it is very important to God who wins. If I contend that the purpose of the game of life is to win, how could I not believe that our winning is important to Him? So my conclusion is that God wants us to be winners in both games—football and life.

You may ask how this could be. "Someone has to lose?" Those guys on the losing team may even seem to be nicer and better Christians than those on the winning side. Here I find myself again venturing into a realm in which I hold neither a degree nor special credentials, so you certainly have the right to a different opinion. But I cannot believe that our heavenly Father desires less for His children than we do for ours. I always want my kids to be winners, and I imagine you do too. But how can you reconcile all this winning and losing? This is the way I have resolved it in my own finite mind.

Over the years, I have attended many sporting events in which both my children and grandchildren have played—some they won and some they lost. However, I never remember any of them being losers; I always considered them winners. You see, in my case as a father and grandfather, my definition of a winner is not measured solely on the scoreboard but rather in the commitment, effort, and sportsmanship exhibited on the field. I don't know if God is a football fan or has a favorite team. But I do know that He loves His children more than we can even comprehend. So I can only imagine how He—a holy, loving, heavenly Father— must feel when He watches His children play in this most important game: life.

However, I would not want you to conclude that a winning score is not important to me. My friends will all attest to the fact that I am one of the most competitive individuals that they know. As a result, when competing in an athletic event, I not only desired to follow the rules of good sportsmanship but also receive the winner's trophy. Likewise, I believe that God wants His children to exhibit similar attributes (His commandments actually spell out the rules) and to also receive the ultimate reward in their game of life. In fact, He guarantees victory.

When discussing the concept of winning, my good friend Richard made the observation that we tend to use the wrong scoring system in our games or, as he put it, "keep the wrong score." It made me think. What if a football team was more focused on its uniforms than its preparation, on individual statistics than its execution, or on anticipated accolades than successfully completing the game? I believe that winning the game would be in jeopardy.

Several years ago, there was a popular bumper sticker that read, "The one who finishes with the most toys wins!" Of course, this was referencing today's emphasis on materialism and the priorities that our society promotes with much fervor. I think Richard has a point. We often view life's scoreboard through faulty bifocals where the prescriptions for long-sightedness/shortsightedness are reversed. When we view those things that are truly important to be less and those things that are unimportant to be more, the outcome of the game of life can also be in jeopardy.

★★★★★★★★★★

*... we tend to use the wrong scoring system
in our games ...*

★★★★★★★★★★

After listening to all this philosophical analysis, you may feel that all this is getting too deep; and to be honest, I can get lost in it too. So let me attempt to bring some clarity to my thinking and explanation by sharing an experience that I had several years back.

A conference championship football game was going to be televised on a Saturday afternoon when I was scheduled to be at a meeting out of town. The winner would play in the national championship game a few weeks later. One of the teams was my very favorite, and I wanted more than anything to see the game. I checked and found out that the game was to be replayed the following Monday evening. So I decided not to read the sports page or watch the sports news that evening, and I instructed my family members not to tell me who won. I was really looking forward to watching this all-important contest, even though it had already been played and the championship had been decided.

Unfortunately, on Sunday evening as I was, what my wife calls, surfing, I passed the sports channel on television. At that very point in time, the little line that crosses the bottom of the screen showed the score of the game that I had planned to watch the next evening. Devastated might be too strong and disappointed too weak to describe my feelings at that moment. Fortunately, the score showed my team winning a close game, but now all the excitement would be gone. Still, I chose to go ahead and watch the game on Monday night. As the game progressed, it didn't transpire like I expected. Actually, my team fell further and further behind. In fact, it played so poorly the first half and into the third quarter that I figured I had misread the score. It must have been backward or maybe from another game. Watching became more difficult because I had gone from what I knew was a sure win to the agony of an unexpected loss. However, just after the four fingers were extended to begin the fourth quarter, my team came alive. Offensively and defensively, that team played its best quarter of the season and miraculously fought its way back to an exciting victory. It was decided on the very last play of the game by a successful field goal. The score turned out to be the exact one that I had seen while surfing. This was an unusual and exciting experience. But more than that, it was a great spiritual lesson for me.

I believe the game of life is like my experience with this important championship football game. Just as I knew, we Christians already know the final score. The winning play actually took place before our own personal game even started. This deciding play exhibited tremendous courage, determination, and sacrifice; we know it today as the greatest play ever executed on earth—our playing field. But instead of a kick through a metal goal post, it occurred on a wooden post—a cross! On that old, rugged cross, Jesus Christ died for us and rose from the dead so that we might have life, both abundantly and eternally—victory!

As our individual games of life are played, we as Christians can be assured that we are a part of the winning team. Our game will include suffering, perseverance, character building, hope, faith, and love. But, by the grace of God, we are already assured of victory. *The fourth quarter ends*; we win the conference (earthly) championship, and in so doing move on to the biggest event of all. It will not occur here on our old playing field and is no longer a competition, but instead it is a celebration. It will take place in an arena so big and beautiful we cannot imagine. Our new home field is called *heaven,* where for eternity we celebrate our victory in Jesus.

But I must remind you that there is one requirement to be assured of the victory. *You must believe.* I *believe* this with all my heart! Now share your beliefs and your heart.

> "We will shout for joy when you are
> **victorious** and will lift up our banners in
> the name of our God" (Psalm 20:5).

Winning: The Replay – Self-Analysis

1. Have you accepted Jesus Christ as your Savior and Lord? Share.

2. Do you realize that the game of life is not won by your efforts but by Christ's sacrifice? How does this change your game plan?

3. In the course of your busy and demanding life, do you sometime forget the game has already been won? If so, what helps you remember this truth?

4. If you truly believe all of this, are you sharing this good news with others? How?

5. Are your priorities focused on the important or unimportant things of life? Explain. If you are in the fourth quarter (even in the two-minute warning or overtime), there is still time to secure the victory and receive the gift of salvation! Do you believe?

ACKNOWLEDGMENTS

My thanks to each of you for taking time to hear me out and for giving thought to this most important event in which we all are participating: *the game of life.* I have attempted to share my heart with you, and I personally have benefited tremendously from the many conversations that I have had with some of you on this subject. I don't see the end to this discussion occurring with the end of this reading; there are so many more related questions that beg for answers. The game continues, and particularly for those of us in the fourth quarter, victory is in sight.

I challenge each of you to share your insights and revelations with others as you complete the game and live out your purpose in life. I personally would welcome your thoughts. Let's visit again.

As a reminder, here is the *purpose* as I see it.

Purpose

The First Quarter	**Learning**
The Second Quarter	**Earning**
Halftime	**Midlife**
The Third Quarter	**Discerning**
The Fourth Quarter	**Yearning**

★★★★★★★★★★★

The purpose of life is to love God, your neighbor,
and yourself and to receive and respond to
God's love and call.

★★★★★★★★★★★

EPILOGUE

Elizabeth

Now that you have read my book, you probably realize what an impact my mother, Elizabeth, had on my life as well as on the lives of many others. Two weeks after submitting this manuscript to the publisher, Mom died peacefully in a nursing home. This is significant to me because her direct influence motivated me to put these ideas in writing. She had indicated that she wanted to write a sequel to her little children's book, *Who I'd Like to Be*. Due to her physical and mental condition, we all knew that this was not going to happen. So one day I told her that I would write a book for both of us. Neither she nor I realized at the time that she would be one of the main characters in *Purpose in the Fourth Quarter*.

What a special lady she was! Through her words and actions, she demonstrated her love for God and others. Below are just a few of the principles that I watched her preach and practice.

- Family should always be among one's top priorities.
- Bloom where you're planted.
- Look for good in every situation.
- Leave a good impression wherever you go.
- Help others reach their potentials.
- People are more important than things.
- God is great; God is good.
- Love unconditionally!

Her funeral, a celebration, was beautiful. It was held in the Lovely Lane Chapel at Epworth By The Sea, St. Simons Island, Georgia, where she had lived for over thirty years. Two of her close pastor friends conducted the service, and we all sang some of her favorite hymns. Later, we had another celebration in Marietta, Georgia, where she spent the last year and a half of her life. More family and friends gathered. Her book, *Who I'd Like to Be,* was read, after which we all released red (her favorite color) balloons. We watched and cried because we realized that we had the rare privilege of living these many years with one of God's saints!

Mom, you lived every quarter with purpose, but your fourth was one to behold. I love you and will see you again when I finish my game!

Bernie

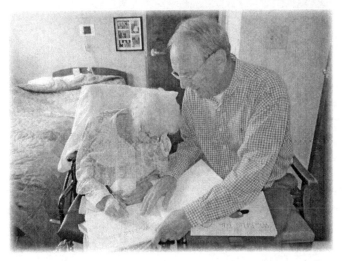

Author with his greatest fan!

ENDNOTES

1   Brown, Bernie. "A Time to Run." 2010.
2   Phillips, Pauline. "Dear Abby." *Marietta Daily Journal,* March 4, 2012, p. D2.
3   With permission from Carolyn Mills.
4   Kock, Kathy. "A Conversation with Dr. Kathy Koch," *In Touch* (Atlanta, Georgia), p. 19.
5   Pine, Chris. Movie review by Davia L. Mosley. *Marietta Daily Journal,* June 29, 2012, p. D1.
6   Warren, Rick. "What on Earth Am I Here For?" From *The Purpose Driven Life.* Grand Rapids, Michigan: Zondervan, 2004, p. 5–7.
7   Brown, Bernie and Snookie. "Bridging the Gap." 2008.

Bernie Brown is also the author of
LESSONS LEARNED ON THE WAY DOWN
A Perspective on Christian Leadership in a Secular World
Visit www.purposeinthefourthquarter.com
Author's E-mail address: bernielb@bellsouth.net

CPSIA information can be obtained at www.ICGtesting.com
Printed in the USA
LVOW060729290313

326566LV00005B/73/P